Endgame

A PLAY IN ONE ACT

FOLLOWED BY

Act Without Words
A MIME FOR ONE PLAYER

By

Samuel Beckett
TRANSLATED FROM THE FRENCH
BY THE AUTHOR

GROVE PRESS, INC.   NEW YORK

First Evergreen Edition 1958
40   39   38
ISBN: 0-394-17208-6
Library of Congress Catalog Card Number: 58-5532

Manufactured in the United States of America

GROVE PRESS, INC., 196 West Houston Street,
New York, N.Y. 10014

For Roger Blin

Endgame

A PLAY IN ONE ACT

THE CHARACTERS:

      NAGG

      NELL

      HAMM

      CLOV

Fin de Partie was first performed at the Royal Court Theatre in London on April 3, 1957. It was directed by Roger Blin, and the décor was designed by Jacques Noel.

Hamm	Roger Blin
Clov	Jean Martin
Nagg	Georges Adet
Nell	Christine Tsingos

Acte sans Paroles was first performed at the Royal Court Theatre in London on April 3, 1957. It was directed and performed by Deryk Mendel, the décor was designed by Jacques Noel and the music composed by John Beckett.

Bare interior.

Grey light.

Left and right back, high up, two small windows, curtains drawn.

Front right, a door. Hanging near door, its face to wall, a picture.

Front left, touching each other, covered with an old sheet, two ashbins.

Center, in an armchair on castors, covered with an old sheet, Hamm.

Motionless by the door, his eyes fixed on Hamm, Clov. Very red face.

Brief tableau.

Clov goes and stands under window left. Stiff, staggering walk. He looks up at window left. He turns and looks at window right. He goes and stands under window right. He looks up at window right. He turns and looks at window left. He goes out, comes back immediately with a small step-ladder, carries it over and sets it down under window left, gets up on it, draws back curtain. He gets down, takes six steps (for example) towards window right, goes back for ladder, carries it over and sets it down under window right, gets up on it, draws back curtain. He gets down, takes three steps towards window left, goes back for ladder, carries it over and sets it down under window left, gets up on it, looks out of window. Brief laugh. He gets down, takes one step towards window right, goes back for ladder, carries it over and sets it down under window right, gets up on it, looks out of window. Brief laugh. He gets down, goes with ladder towards ashbins, halts, turns, carries back ladder and sets it down under window right, goes to ashbins, removes sheet covering them, folds it over his arm. He raises one lid, stoops and looks into bin. Brief laugh. He closes lid. Same with other bin. He goes to Hamm, removes sheet covering him, folds it over his arm. In a dressing-gown, a stiff toque on his head, a large blood-stained handkerchief over his face, a whistle hanging from his neck, a rug over his knees, thick socks on his feet, Hamm seems to be asleep. Clov looks him over. Brief laugh. He goes to door, halts, turns towards auditorium.

CLOV *(fixed gaze, tonelessly)*:
Finished, it's finished, nearly finished, it must be nearly finished.
(Pause.)
Grain upon grain, one by one, and one day, suddenly, there's a heap, a little heap, the impossible heap.
(Pause.)
I can't be punished any more.

1

(Pause.)

I'll go now to my kitchen, ten feet by ten feet by ten feet, and wait for him to whistle me.

(Pause.)

Nice dimensions, nice proportions, I'll lean on the table, and look at the wall, and wait for him to whistle me.

(He remains a moment motionless, then goes out. He comes back immediately, goes to window right, takes up the ladder and carries it out. Pause. Hamm stirs. He yawns under the handkerchief. He removes the handkerchief from his face. Very red face. Black glasses.)

HAMM:

Me—

(he yawns)

—to play.

(He holds the handkerchief spread out before him.)

Old stancher!

(He takes off his glasses, wipes his eyes, his face, the glasses, puts them on again, folds the handkerchief and puts it back neatly in the breast-pocket of his dressing-gown. He clears his throat, joins the tips of his fingers.)

Can there be misery—

(he yawns)

—loftier than mine? No doubt. Formerly. But now?

(Pause.)

My father?

(Pause.)

My mother?

(Pause.)

My . . . dog?

(Pause.)

Oh I am willing to believe they suffer as much as such creatures can suffer. But does that mean their sufferings equal mine? No doubt.

(Pause.)

No, all is a—

(he yawns)

—bsolute,

(proudly)

the bigger a man is the fuller he is.
(Pause. Gloomily.)
And the emptier.
(He sniffs.)
Clov!
(Pause.)
No, alone.
(Pause.)
What dreams! Those forests!
(Pause.)
Enough, it's time it ended, in the shelter too.
(Pause.)
And yet I hesitate, I hesitate to . . . to end. Yes, there it is, it's time it ended and yet I hesitate to—
(he yawns)
—to end.
(Yawns.)
God, I'm tired, i'd be better off in bed.
(He whistles. Enter Clov immediately. He halts beside the chair.)
You pollute the air!
(Pause.)
Get me ready, I'm going to bed.

CLOV:

I've just got you up.

HAMM:

And what of it?

CLOV:

I can't be getting you up and putting you to bed every five minutes, I have things to do.
(Pause.)

HAMM:

Did you ever see my eyes?

CLOV:

No.

HAMM:

Did you never have the curiosity, while I was sleeping, to take off my glasses and look at my eyes?

3

CLOV:
Pulling back the lids?
(Pause.)
No.

HAMM:
One of these days I'll show them to you.
(Pause.)
It seems they've gone all white.
(Pause.)
What time is it?

CLOV:
The same as usual.

HAMM (gesture towards window right):
Have you looked?

CLOV:
Yes.

HAMM:
Well?

CLOV:
Zero.

HAMM:
It'd need to rain.

CLOV:
It won't rain.
(Pause.)

HAMM:
Apart from that, how do you feel?

CLOV:
I don't complain.

HAMM:
You feel normal?

CLOV (irritably):
I tell you I don't complain.

HAMM:
I feel a little queer.
(Pause.)

4

Clov!

CLOV:

Yes.

HAMM:

Have you not had enough?

CLOV:

Yes!

(Pause.)

Of what?

HAMM:

Of this . . . this . . . thing.

CLOV:

I always had.

(Pause.)

Not you?

HAMM *(gloomily)*:

Then there's no reason for it to change.

CLOV:

It may end.

(Pause.)

All life long the same questions, the same answers.

HAMM:

Get me ready.

(Clov does not move.)

Go and get the sheet.

(Clov does not move.)

Clov!

CLOV:

Yes.

HAMM:

I'll give you nothing more to eat.

CLOV:

Then we'll die.

HAMM:

I'll give you just enough to keep you from dying. You'll be hungry all the time.

5

CLOV:
  Then we won't die.
  (Pause.)
  I'll go and get the sheet.
  (He goes towards the door.)

HAMM:
  No!
  (Clov halts.)
  I'll give you one biscuit per day.
  (Pause.)
  One and a half.
  (Pause.)
  Why do you stay with me?

CLOV:
  Why do you keep me?

HAMM:
  There's no one else.

CLOV:
  There's nowhere else.
  (Pause.)

HAMM:
  You're leaving me all the same.

CLOV:
  I'm trying.

HAMM:
  You don't love me.

CLOV:
  No.

HAMM:
  You loved me once.

CLOV:
  Once!

HAMM:
  I've made you suffer too much.
  (Pause.)
  Haven't I?

6

CLOV:

　It's not that.

HAMM (*shocked*):

　I haven't made you suffer too much?

CLOV:

　Yes!

HAMM (*relieved*):

　Ah you gave me a fright!
　(*Pause. Coldly.*)
　Forgive me.
　(*Pause. Louder.*)
　I said, Forgive me.

CLOV:

　I heard you.
　(*Pause.*)
　Have you bled?

HAMM:

　Less.
　(*Pause.*)
　Is it not time for my pain-killer?

CLOV:

　No.
　(*Pause.*)

HAMM:

　How are your eyes?

CLOV:

　Bad.

HAMM:

　How are your legs?

CLOV:

　Bad.

HAMM:

　But you can move.

CLOV:

　Yes.

HAMM (violently):
   Then move!
   (Clov goes to back wall, leans against it with his forehead and hands.)
   Where are you?

CLOV:
   Here.

HAMM:
   Come back!
   (Clov returns to his place beside the chair.)
   Where are you?

CLOV:
   Here.

HAMM:
   Why don't you kill me?

CLOV:
   I don't know the combination of the cupboard.
   (Pause.)

HAMM:
   Go and get two bicycle-wheels.

CLOV:
   There are no more bicycle-wheels.

HAMM:
   What have you done with your bicycle?

CLOV:
   I never had a bicycle.

HAMM:
   The thing is impossible.

CLOV:
   When there were still bicycles I wept to have one. I crawled
   at your feet. You told me to go to hell. Now there are none.

HAMM:
   And your rounds? When you inspected my paupers. Always
   on foot?

CLOV:
   Sometimes on horse.
   (The lid of one of the bins lifts and the hands of Nagg appear, gripping

8

the rim. Then his head emerges. Nightcap. Very white face. Nagg yawns, then listens.)
I'll leave you, I have things to do.

HAMM:
In your kitchen?

CLOV:
Yes.

HAMM:
Outside of here it's death.
(Pause.)
All right, be off.
(Exit Clov. Pause.)
We're getting on.

NAGG:
Me pap!

HAMM:
Accursed progenitor!

NAGG:
Me pap!

HAMM:
The old folks at home! No decency left! Guzzle, guzzle, that's all they think of.
(He whistles. Enter Clov. He halts beside the chair.)
Well! I thought you were leaving me.

CLOV:
Oh not just yet, not just yet.

NAGG:
Me pap!

HAMM:
Give him his pap.

CLOV:
There's no more pap.

HAMM *(to Nagg)*:
Do you hear that? There's no more pap. You'll never get any more pap.

9

NAGG:

    I want me pap!

HAMM:

    Give him a biscuit.

    (Exit Clov.)

    Accursed fornicator! How are your stumps?

NAGG:

    Never mind me stumps.

    (Enter Clov with biscuit.)

CLOV:

    I'm back again, with the biscuit.

    (He gives biscuit to Nagg who fingers it, sniffs it.)

NAGG *(plaintively)*:

    What is it?

CLOV:

    Spratt's medium.

NAGG *(as before)*:

    It's hard! I can't!

HAMM:

    Bottle him!

    (Clov pushes Nagg back into the bin, closes the lid.)

CLOV *(returning to his place beside the chair)*:

    If age but knew!

HAMM:

    Sit on him!

CLOV:

    I can't sit.

HAMM:

    True. And I can't stand.

CLOV:

    So it is.

HAMM:

    Every man his speciality.

    (Pause.)

    No phone calls?

(Pause.)
Don't we laugh?

CLOV *(after reflection)*:
I don't feel like it.

HAMM *(after reflection)*:
Nor I.
(Pause.)
Clov!

CLOV:
Yes.

HAMM:
Nature has forgotten us.

CLOV:
There's no more nature.

HAMM:
No more nature! You exaggerate.

CLOV:
In the vicinity.

HAMM:
But we breathe, we change! We lose our hair, our teeth! Our bloom! Our ideals!

CLOV:
Then she hasn't forgotten us.

HAMM:
But you say there is none.

CLOV *(sadly)*:
No one that ever lived ever thought so crooked as we.

HAMM:
We do what we can.

CLOV:
We shouldn't.
(Pause.)

HAMM:
You're a bit of all right, aren't you?

CLOV:

    A smithereen.

    (Pause.)

HAMM:

    This is slow work.

    (Pause.)

    Is it not time for my pain-killer?

CLOV:

    No.

    (Pause.)

    I'll leave you, I have things to do.

HAMM:

    In your kitchen?

CLOV:

    Yes.

HAMM:

    What, I'd like to know.

CLOV:

    I look at the wall.

HAMM:

    The wall! And what do you see on your wall? Mene, mene? Naked bodies?

CLOV:

    I see my light dying.

HAMM:

    Your light dying! Listen to that! Well, it can die just as well here, *your* light. Take a look at me and then come back and tell me what you think of *your* light.

    (Pause.)

CLOV:

    You shouldn't speak to me like that.

    (Pause.)

HAMM *(coldly)*:

    Forgive me.

    (Pause. Louder.)

    I said, Forgive me.

12

CLOV:
  I heard you.
  (The lid of Nagg's bin lifts. His hands appear, gripping the rim. Then his head emerges. In his mouth the biscuit. He listens.)

HAMM:
  Did your seeds come up?

CLOV:
  No.

HAMM:
  Did you scratch round them to see if they had sprouted?

CLOV:
  They haven't sprouted.

HAMM:
  Perhaps it's still too early.

CLOV:
  If they were going to sprout they would have sprouted.
  (Violently.)
  They'll never sprout!
  (Pause. Nagg takes biscuit in his hand.)

HAMM:
  This is not much fun.
  (Pause.)
  But that's always the way at the end of the day, isn't it, Clov?

CLOV:
  Always.

HAMM:
  It's the end of the day like any other day, isn't it, Clov?

CLOV:
  Looks like it.
  (Pause.)

HAMM *(anguished)*:
  What's happening, what's happening?

CLOV:
  Something is taking its course.
  (Pause.)

13

HAMM:
    All right, be off.
    (*He leans back in his chair, remains motionless. Clov does not move, heaves a great groaning sigh. Hamm sits up.*)
    I thought I told you to be off.

CLOV:
    I'm trying.
    (*He goes to door, halts.*)
    Ever since I was whelped.
    (*Exit Clov.*)

HAMM:
    We're getting on.
    (*He leans back in his chair, remains motionless. Nagg knocks on the lid of the other bin. Pause. He knocks harder. The lid lifts and the hands of Nell appear, gripping the rim. Then her head emerges. Lace cap. Very white face.*)

NELL:
    What is it, my pet?
    (*Pause.*)
    Time for love?

NAGG:
    Were you asleep?

NELL:
    Oh no!

NAGG:
    Kiss me.

NELL:
    We can't.

NAGG:
    Try.
    (*Their heads strain towards each other, fail to meet, fall apart again.*)

NELL:
    Why this farce, day after day?
    (*Pause.*)

NAGG:
    I've lost me tooth.

14

NELL:
  When?
NAGG:
  I had it yesterday.
NELL *(elegiac)*:
  Ah yesterday!
  (They turn painfully towards each other.)
NAGG:
  Can you see me?
NELL:
  Hardly. And you?
NAGG:
  What?
NELL:
  Can you see me?
NAGG:
  Hardly.
NELL:
  So much the better, so much the better.
NAGG:
  Don't say that.
  (Pause.)
  Our sight has failed.
NELL:
  Yes.
  (Pause. They turn away from each other.)
NAGG:
  Can you hear me?
NELL:
  Yes. And you?
NAGG:
  Yes.
  (Pause.)
  Our hearing hasn't failed.
NELL:
  Our what?

15

NAGG:
  Our hearing.

NELL:
  No.
  (Pause.)
  Have you anything else to say to me?

NAGG:
  Do you remember—

NELL:
  No.

NAGG:
  When we crashed on our tandem and lost our shanks.
  (They laugh heartily.)

NELL:
  It was in the Ardennes.
  (They laugh less heartily.)

NAGG:
  On the road to Sedan.
  (They laugh still less heartily.)
  Are you cold?

NELL:
  Yes, perished. And you?

NAGG:
  (Pause.)
  I'm freezing.
  (Pause.)
  Do you want to go in?

NELL:
  Yes.

NAGG:
  Then go in.
  (Nell does not move)
  Why don't you go in?

NELL:
  I don't know.
  (Pause.)

16

NAGG:
Has he changed your sawdust?

NELL:
It isn't sawdust.
(Pause. Wearily.)
Can you not be a little accurate, Nagg?

NAGG:
Your sand then. It's not important.

NELL:
It is important.
(Pause.)

NAGG:
It was sawdust once.

NELL:
Once!

NAGG:
And now it's sand.
(Pause.)
From the shore.
(Pause. Impatiently.)
Now it's sand he fetches from the shore.

NELL:
Now it's sand.

NAGG:
Has he changed yours?

NELL:
No.

NAGG:
Nor mine.
(Pause.)
I won't have it!
(Pause. Holding up the biscuit.)
Do you want a bit?

NELL:
No.

17

(Pause.)
Of what?

NAGG:
   Biscuit. I've kept you half.
   (He looks at the biscuit. Proudly.)
   Three quarters. For you. Here.
   (He proffers the biscuit.)
   No?
   (Pause.)
   Do you not feel well?

HAMM *(wearily)*:
   Quiet, quiet, you're keeping me awake.
   (Pause.)
   Talk softer.
   (Pause.)
   If I could sleep I might make love. I'd go into the woods. My
   eyes would see . . . the sky, the earth. I'd run, run, they
   wouldn't catch me.
   (Pause.)
   Nature!
   (Pause.)
   There's something dripping in my head.
   (Pause.)
   A heart, a heart in my head.
   (Pause.)

NAGG *(soft)*:
   Do you hear him? A heart in his head!
   (He chuckles cautiously.)

NELL:
   One mustn't laugh at those things, Nagg. Why must you always laugh at them?

NAGG:
   Not so loud!

NELL *(without lowering her voice)*:
   Nothing is funnier than unhappiness, I grant you that. But—

NAGG *(shocked)*:
   Oh!

18

NELL:

Yes, yes, it's the most comical thing in the world. And we laugh, we laugh, with a will, in the beginning. But it's always the same thing. Yes, it's like the funny story we have heard too often, we still find it funny, but we don't laugh any more.
(Pause.)
Have you anything else to say to me?

NAGG:

No.

NELL:

Are you quite sure?
(Pause.)
Then I'll leave you.

NAGG:

Do you not want your biscuit?
(Pause.)
I'll keep it for you.
(Pause.)
I thought you were going to leave me.

NELL:

I am going to leave you.

NAGG:

Could you give me a scratch before you go?

NELL:

No.
(Pause.)
Where?

NAGG:

In the back.

NELL:

No.
(Pause.)
Rub yourself against the rim.

NAGG:

It's lower down. In the hollow.

19

NELL:
  What hollow?

NAGG:
  The hollow!
  (Pause.)
  Could you not?
  (Pause.)
  Yesterday you scratched me there.

NELL *(elegiac)*:
  Ah yesterday!

NAGG:
  Could you not?
  (Pause.)
  Would you like me to scratch you?
  (Pause.)
  Are you crying again?

NELL:
  I was trying.
  (Pause.)

HAMM:
  Perhaps it's a little vein.
  (Pause.)

NAGG:
  What was that he said?

NELL:
  Perhaps it's a little vein.

NAGG:
  What does that mean?
  (Pause.)
  That means nothing.
  (Pause.)
  Will I tell you the story of the tailor?

NELL:
  No.
  (Pause.)
  What for?

NAGG:
   To cheer you up.
NELL:
   It's not funny.
NAGG:
   It always made you laugh.
   (Pause.)
   The first time I thought you'd die.
NELL:
   It was on Lake Como.
   (Pause.)
   One April afternoon.
   (Pause.)
   Can you believe it?
NAGG:
   What?
NELL:
   That we once went out rowing on Lake Como.
   (Pause.)
   One April afternoon.
NAGG:
   We had got engaged the day before.
NELL:
   Engaged!
NAGG:
   You were in such fits that we capsized. By rights we should
   have been drowned.
NELL:
   It was because I felt happy.
NAGG *(indignant)*:
   It was not, it was not, it was my story and nothing else. Happy!
   Don't you laugh at it still? Every time I tell it. Happy!
NELL:
   It was deep, deep. And you could see down to the bottom.
   So white. So clean.

21

NAGG:

Let me tell it again.

(Raconteur's voice.)

An Englishman, needing a pair of striped trousers in a hurry for the New Year festivities, goes to his tailor who takes his measurements.

(Tailor's voice.)

"That's the lot, come back in four days, I'll have it ready." Good. Four days later.

(Tailor's voice.)

"So sorry, come back in a week, I've made a mess of the seat." Good, that's all right, a neat seat can be very ticklish. A week later.

(Tailor's voice.)

"Frightfully sorry, come back in ten days, I've made a hash of the crotch." Good, can't be helped, a snug crotch is always a teaser. Ten days later.

(Tailor's voice.)

"Dreadfully sorry, come back in a fortnight, I've made a balls of the fly." Good, at a pinch, a smart fly is a stiff proposition.

(Pause. Normal voice.)

I never told it worse.

(Pause. Gloomy.)

I tell this story worse and worse.

(Pause. Raconteur's voice.)

Well, to make it short, the bluebells are blowing and he ballockses the buttonholes.

(Customer's voice.)

"God damn you to hell, Sir, no, it's indecent, there are limits! In six days, do you hear me, six days, God made the world. Yes Sir, no less Sir, the WORLD! And you are not bloody well capable of making me a pair of trousers in three months!"

(Tailor's voice, scandalized.)

"But my dear Sir, my dear Sir, look—

(disdainful gesture, disgustedly)

—at the world—

(pause)

22

and look—
(loving gesture, proudly)
—at my TROUSERS!"
(Pause. He looks at Nell who has remained impassive, her eyes unseeing, breaks into a high forced laugh, cuts it short, pokes his head towards Nell, launches his laugh again.)

HAMM:
   Silence!
   (Nagg starts, cuts short his laugh.)

NELL:
   You could see down to the bottom.

HAMM *(exasperated)*:
   Have you not finished? Will you never finish?
   (With sudden fury.)
   Will this never finish?
   (Nagg disappears into his bin, closes the lid behind him. Nell does not move. Frenziedly.)
   My kingdom for a nightman!
   (He whistles. Enter Clov.)
   Clear away this muck! Chuck it in the sea!
   (Clov goes to bins, halts.)

NELL:
   So white.

HAMM:
   What? What's she blathering about?
   (Clov stoops, takes Nell's hand, feels her pulse.)

NELL *(to Clov)*:
   Desert!
   (Clov lets go her hand, pushes her back in the bin, closes the lid.)

CLOV *(returning to his place beside the chair)*:
   She has no pulse.

HAMM:
   What was she drivelling about?

CLOV:
   She told me to go away, into the desert.

HAMM:
   Damn busybody! Is that all?

23

CLOV:
  No.

HAMM:
  What else?

CLOV:
  I didn't understand.

HAMM:
  Have you bottled her?

CLOV:
  Yes.

HAMM:
  Are they both bottled?

CLOV:
  Yes.

HAMM:
  Screw down the lids.
  (Clov goes towards door.)
  Time enough.
  (Clov halts.)
  My anger subsides, I'd like to pee.

CLOV *(with alacrity)*:
  I'll go and get the catheter.
  (He goes towards door.)

HAMM:
  Time enough.
  (Clov halts.)
  Give me my pain-killer.

CLOV:
  It's too soon.
  (Pause.)
  It's too soon on top of your tonic, it wouldn't act.

HAMM:
  In the morning they brace you up and in the evening they
  calm you down. Unless it's the other way round.
  (Pause.)
  That old doctor, he's dead naturally?

CLOV:
  He wasn't old.
HAMM:
  But he's dead?
CLOV:
  Naturally.
  (Pause.)
  You ask *me* that?
  (Pause.)
HAMM:
  Take me for a little turn.
  (Clov goes behind the chair and pushes it forward.)
  Not too fast!
  (Clov pushes chair.)
  Right round the world!
  (Clov pushes chair.)
  Hug the walls, then back to the center again.
  (Clov pushes chair.)
  I was right in the center, wasn't I?
CLOV *(pushing)*:
  Yes.
HAMM:
  We'd need a proper wheel-chair. With big wheels. Bicycle wheels!
  (Pause.)
  Are you hugging?
CLOV *(pushing)*:
  Yes.
HAMM *(groping for wall)*:
  It's a lie! Why do you lie to me?
CLOV *(bearing closer to wall)*:
  There! There!
HAMM:
  Stop!
  (Clov stops chair close to back wall. Hamm lays his hand against wall.)
  Old wall!

25

(Pause.)
Beyond is the . . . other hell.
(Pause. Violently.)
Closer! Closer! Up against!

CLOV:
Take away your hand.
(Hamm withdraws his hand. Clov rams chair against wall.)
There!
(Hamm leans towards wall, applies his ear to it.)

HAMM:
Do you hear?
(He strikes the wall with his knuckles.)
Do you hear? Hollow bricks!
(He strikes again.)
All that's hollow!
(Pause. He straightens up. Violently.)
That's enough. Back!

CLOV:
We haven't done the round.

HAMM:
Back to my place!
(Clov pushes chair back to center.)
Is that my place?

CLOV:
Yes, that's your place.

HAMM:
Am I right in the center?

CLOV:
I'll measure it.

HAMM:
More or less! More or less!

CLOV *(moving chair slightly)*:
There!

HAMM:
I'm more or less in the center?

CLOV:
  I'd say so.

HAMM:
  You'd say so! Put me right in the center!

CLOV:
  I'll go and get the tape.

HAMM:
  Roughly! Roughly!
  (Clov moves chair slightly.)
  Bang in the center!

CLOV:
  There!
  (Pause.)

HAMM:
  I feel a little too far to the left.
  (Clov moves chair slightly.)
  Now I feel a little too far to the right.
  (Clov moves chair slightly.)
  I feel a little too far forward.
  (Clov moves chair slightly.)
  Now I feel a little too far back.
  (Clov moves chair slightly.)
  Don't stay there,
  (i.e. behind the chair).
  you give me the shivers.
  (Clov returns to his place beside the chair.)

CLOV:
  If I could kill him I'd die happy.
  (Pause.)

HAMM:
  What's the weather like?

CLOV:
  As usual.

HAMM:
  Look at the earth.

CLOV:
    I've looked.

HAMM:
    With the glass?

CLOV:
    No need of the glass.

HAMM:
    Look at it with the glass.

CLOV:
    I'll go and get the glass.
    (Exit Clov.)

HAMM:
    No need of the glass!
    (Enter Clov with telescope.)

CLOV:
    I'm back again, with the glass.
    (He goes to window right, looks up at it.)
    I need the steps.

HAMM:
    Why? Have you shrunk?
    (Exit Clov with telescope.)
    I don't like that, I don't like that.
    (Enter Clov with ladder, but without telescope.)

CLOV:
    I'm back again, with the steps.
    (He sets down ladder under window right, gets up on it, realizes he has not the telescope, gets down.)
    I need the glass.
    (He goes towards door.)

HAMM *(violently)*:
    But you have the glass!

CLOV *(halting, violently)*:
    No, I haven't the glass!
    (Exit Clov.)

HAMM:
    This is deadly.

28

(Enter Clov with telescope. He goes towards ladder.)

CLOV:

Things are livening up.
(He gets up on ladder, raises the telescope, lets it fall.)
I did it on purpose.
(He gets down, picks up the telescope, turns it on auditorium.)
I see . . . a multitude . . . in transports . . . of joy.
(Pause.)
That's what I call a magnifier.
(He lowers the telescope, turns towards Hamm.)
Well? Don't we laugh?

HAMM *(after reflection)*:

I don't.

CLOV *(after reflection)*:

Nor I.
(He gets up on ladder, turns the telescope on the without.)
Let's see.
(He looks, moving the telescope.)
Zero . . .
(he looks)
. . . zero . . .
(he looks)
. . . and zero.

HAMM:

Nothing stirs. All is—

CLOV:

Zer—

HAMM *(violently)*:

Wait till you're spoken to!
(Normal voice.)
All is . . . all is . . . all is what?
(Violently.)
All is what?

CLOV:

What all is? In a word? Is that what you want to know? Just a moment.

29

(He turns the telescope on the without, looks, lowers the telescope, turns towards Hamm.)
Corpsed.
(Pause.)
Well? Content?

HAMM:
Look at the sea.

CLOV:
It's the same.

HAMM:
Look at the ocean!
(Clov gets down, takes a few steps towards window left, goes back for ladder, carries it over and sets it down under window left, gets up on it, turns the telescope on the without, looks at length. He starts, lowers the telescope, examines it, turns it again on the without.)

CLOV:
Never seen anything like that!

HAMM *(anxious)*:
What? A sail? A fin? Smoke?

CLOV *(looking)*:
The light is sunk.

HAMM *(relieved)*:
Pah! We all knew that.

CLOV *(looking)*:
There was a bit left.

HAMM:
The base.

CLOV *(looking)*:
Yes.

HAMM:
And now?

CLOV *(looking)*:
All gone.

HAMM:
No gulls?

CLOV *(looking)*:
  Gulls!

HAMM:
  And the horizon? Nothing on the horizon?

CLOV *(lowering the telescope, turning towards Hamm, exasperated)*:
  What in God's name could there be on the horizon?
  (Pause.)

HAMM:
  The waves, how are the waves?

CLOV:
  The waves?
  (He turns the telescope on the waves.)
  Lead.

HAMM:
  And the sun?

CLOV *(looking)*:
  Zero.

HAMM:
  But it should be sinking. Look again.

CLOV *(looking)*:
  Damn the sun.

HAMM:
  Is it night already then?

CLOV *(looking)*:
  No.

HAMM:
  Then what is it?

CLOV *(looking)*:
  Gray.
  (Lowering the telescope, turning towards Hamm, louder.)
  Gray!
  (Pause. Still louder.)
  GRRAY!
  (Pause. He gets down, approaches Hamm from behind, whispers in his ear.)

31

HAMM (*starting*):
Gray! Did I hear you say gray?

CLOV:
Light black. From pole to pole.

HAMM:
You exaggerate.
(*Pause.*)
Don't stay there, you give me the shivers.
(*Clov returns to his place beside the chair.*)

CLOV:
Why this farce, day after day?

HAMM:
Routine. One never knows.
(*Pause.*)
Last night I saw inside my breast. There was a big sore.

CLOV:
Pah! You saw your heart.

HAMM:
No, it was living.
(*Pause. Anquished.*)
Clov!

CLOV:
Yes.

HAMM:
What's happening?

CLOV:
Something is taking its course.
(*Pause.*)

HAMM:
Clov!

CLOV (*impatiently*):
What is it?

HAMM:
We're not beginning to . . . to . . . mean something?

CLOV:

Mean something! You and I, mean something!
(Brief laugh.)
Ah that's a good one!

HAMM:

I wonder.
(Pause.)
Imagine if a rational being came back to earth, wouldn't he be liable to get ideas into his head if he observed us long enough.
(Voice of rational being.)
Ah, good, now I see what it is, yes, now I understand what they're at!
(Clov starts, drops the telescope and begins to scratch his belly with both hands. Normal voice.)
And without going so far as that, we ourselves . . .
(with emotion)
. . . we ourselves . . . at certain moments . . .
(Vehemently.)
To think perhaps it won't all have been for nothing!

CLOV *(anguished, scratching himself)*:

I have a flea!

HAMM:

A flea! Are there still fleas?

CLOV:

On me there's one.
(Scratching.)
Unless it's a crablouse.

HAMM *(very perturbed)*:

But humanity might start from there all over again! Catch him, for the love of God!

CLOV:

I'll go and get the powder.
(Exit Clov.)

HAMM:

A flea! This is awful! What a day!

33

(Enter Clov with a sprinkling-tin.)

CLOV:

I'm back again, with the insecticide.

HAMM:

Let him have it!

(Clov loosens the top of his trousers, pulls it forward and shakes powder into the aperture. He stoops, looks, waits, starts, frenziedly shakes more powder, stoops, looks, waits.)

CLOV:

The bastard!

HAMM:

Did you get him?

CLOV:

Looks like it.

(He drops the tin and adjusts his trousers.)

Unless he's laying doggo.

HAMM:

Laying! Lying you mean. Unless he's *lying* doggo.

CLOV:

Ah? One says lying? One doesn't say laying?

HAMM:

Use your head, can't you. If he was laying we'd be bitched.

CLOV:

Ah.

(Pause.)

What about that pee?

HAMM:

I'm having it.

CLOV:

Ah that's the spirit, that's the spirit!

(Pause.)

HAMM *(with ardour)*:

Let's go from here, the two of us! South! You can make a raft and the currents will carry us away, far away, to other . . . mammals!

CLOV:
    God forbid!

HAMM:
    Alone, I'll embark alone! Get working on that raft immedi-
    ately. Tomorrow I'll be gone for ever.

CLOV *(hastening towards door)*:
    I'll start straight away.

HAMM:
    Wait!
    (Clov halts.)
    Will there be sharks, do you think?

CLOV:
    Sharks? I don't know. If there are there will be.
    (He goes towards door.)

HAMM:
    Wait!
    (Clov halts.)
    Is it not yet time for my pain-killer?

CLOV *(violently)*:
    No!
    (He goes towards door.)

HAMM:
    Wait!
    (Clov halts.)
    How are your eyes?

CLOV:
    Bad.

HAMM:
    But you can see.

CLOV:
    All I want.

HAMM:
    How are your legs?

CLOV:
    Bad.

HAMM:
   But you can walk.

CLOV:
   I come . . . and go.

HAMM:
   In my house.
   (Pause. With prophetic relish.)
   One day you'll be blind, like me. You'll be sitting there, a
   speck in the void, in the dark, for ever, like me.
   (Pause.)
   One day you'll say to yourself, I'm tired, I'll sit down, and
   you'll go and sit down. Then you'll say, I'm hungry, I'll get up
   and get something to eat. But you won't get up. You'll say, I
   shouldn't have sat down, but since I have I'll sit on a little
   longer, then I'll get up and get something to eat. But you
   won't get up and you won't get anything to eat.
   (Pause.)
   You'll look at the wall a while, then you'll say, I'll close my
   eyes, perhaps have a little sleep, after that I'll feel better, and
   you'll close them. And when you open them again there'll be
   no wall any more.
   (Pause.)
   Infinite emptiness will be all around you, all the resurrected
   dead of all the ages wouldn't fill it, and there you'll be like a
   little bit of grit in the middle of the steppe.
   (Pause.)
   Yes, one day you'll know what it is, you'll be like me, except
   that you won't have anyone with you, because you won't have
   had pity on anyone and because there won't be anyone left
   to have pity on.
   (Pause.)

CLOV:
   It's not certain.
   (Pause.)
   And there's one thing you forget.

36

HAMM:
   Ah?

CLOV:
   I can't sit down.

HAMM (*impatiently*):
   Well you'll lie down then, what the hell! Or you'll come to
   a standstill, simply stop and stand still, the way you are now.
   One day you'll say, I'm tired, I'll stop. What does the attitude
   matter?
   (Pause.)

CLOV:
   So you all want me to leave you.

HAMM:
   Naturally.

CLOV:
   Then I'll leave you.

HAMM:
   You can't leave us.

CLOV:
   Then I won't leave you.
   (Pause.)

HAMM:
   Why don't you finish us?
   (Pause.)
   I'll tell you the combination of the cupboard if you promise to
   finish me.

CLOV:
   I couldn't finish you.

HAMM:
   Then you won't finish me.
   (Pause.)

CLOV:
   I'll leave you, I have things to do.

37

HAMM:
Do you remember when you came here?

CLOV:
No. Too small, you told me.

HAMM:
Do you remember your father.

CLOV *(wearily)*:
Same answer.
(Pause.)
You've asked me these questions millions of times.

HAMM:
I love the old questions.
(With fervour.)
Ah the old questions, the old answers, there's nothing like
them!
(Pause.)
It was I was a father to you.

CLOV:
Yes.
(He looks at Hamm fixedly.)
You were that to me.

HAMM:
My house a home for you.

CLOV:
Yes.
(He looks about him.)
This was that for me.

HAMM *(proudly)*:
But for me,
(gesture towards himself)
no father. But for Hamm,
(gesture towards surroundings)
no home.
(Pause.)

CLOV:
I'll leave you.

38

HAMM:
  Did you ever think of one thing?

CLOV:
  Never.

HAMM:
  That here we're down in a hole.
  (Pause.)
  But beyond the hills? Eh? Perhaps it's still green. Eh?
  (Pause.)
  Flora! Pomona!
  (Ecstatically.)
  Ceres!
  (Pause.)
  Perhaps you won't need to go very far.

CLOV:
  I can't go very far.
  (Pause.)
  I'll leave you.

HAMM:
  Is my dog ready?

CLOV:
  He lacks a leg.

HAMM:
  Is he silky?

CLOV:
  He's a kind of Pomeranian.

HAMM:
  Go and get him.

CLOV:
  He lacks a leg.

HAMM:
  Go and get him!
  (Exit Clov.)
  We're getting on.
  (Enter Clov holding by one of its three legs a black toy dog.)

39

CLOV:
   Your dogs are here.
   (He hands the dog to Hamm who feels it, fondles it.)

HAMM:
   He's white, isn't he?

CLOV:
   Nearly.

HAMM:
   What do you mean, nearly? Is he white or isn't he?

CLOV:
   He isn't.
   (Pause.)

HAMM:
   You've forgotten the sex.

CLOV *(vexed)*:
   But he isn't finished. The sex goes on at the end.
   (Pause.)

HAMM:
   You haven't put on his ribbon.

CLOV *(angrily)*:
   But he isn't finished, I tell you! First you finish your dog and
   then you put on his ribbon!
   (Pause.)

HAMM:
   Can he stand?

CLOV:
   I don't know.

HAMM:
   Try.
   (He hands the dog to Clov who places it on the ground.)
   Well?

CLOV:
   Wait!
   *(He squats down and tries to get the dog to stand on its three legs,
   fails, lets it go. The dog falls on its side.)*

HAMM (impatiently):
  Well?

CLOV:
  He's standing.

HAMM (groping for the dog):
  Where? Where is he?
  (Clov holds up the dog in a standing position.)

CLOV:
  There.
  (He takes Hamm's hand and guides it towards the dog's head.)

HAMM (his hand on the dog's head):
  Is he gazing at me?

CLOV:
  Yes.

HAMM (proudly):
  As if he were asking me to take him for a walk?

CLOV:
  If you like.

HAMM (as before):
  Or as if he were begging me for a bone.
  (He withdraws his hand.)
  Leave him like that, standing there imploring me.
  (Clov straightens up. The dog falls on its side.)

CLOV:
  I'll leave you.

HAMM:
  Have you had your visions?

CLOV:
  Less.

HAMM:
  Is Mother Pegg's light on?

CLOV:
  Light! How could anyone's light be on?

41

HAMM:
  Extinguished!
CLOV:
  Naturally it's extinguished. If it's not on it's extinguished.
HAMM:
  No, I mean Mother Pegg.
CLOV:
  But naturally she's extinguished!
  (Pause.)
  What's the matter with you today?
HAMM:
  I'm taking my course.
  (Pause.)
  Is she buried?
CLOV:
  Buried! Who would have buried her?
HAMM:
  You.
CLOV:
  Me! Haven't I enough to do without burying people?
HAMM:
  But you'll bury me.
CLOV:
  No I won't bury you.
  (Pause.)
HAMM:
  She was bonny once, like a flower of the field.
  (With reminiscent leer.)
  And a great one for the men!
CLOV:
  We too were bonny—once. It's a rare thing not to have been bonny—once.
  (Pause.)
HAMM:
  Go and get the gaff.

42

(Clov goes to door, halts.)

CLOV:
Do this, do that, and I do it. I never refuse. Why?

HAMM:
You're not able to.

CLOV:
Soon I won't do it any more.

HAMM:
You won't be able to any more.
(Exit Clov.)
Ah the creatures, the creatures, everything has to be explained to them.
(Enter Clov with gaff.)

CLOV:
Here's your gaff. Stick it up.
(He gives the gaff to Hamm who, wielding it like a puntpole, tries to move his chair.)

HAMM:
Did I move?

CLOV:
No.
(Hamm throws down the gaff.)

HAMM:
Go and get the oilcan.

CLOV:
What for?

HAMM:
To oil the castors.

CLOV:
I oiled them yesterday.

HAMM:
Yesterday! What does that mean? Yesterday!

CLOV *(violently)*:
That means that bloody awful day, long ago, before this bloody

43

awful day. I use the words you taught me. If they don't mean anything any more, teach me others. Or let me be silent.
(Pause.)

HAMM:

I once knew a madman who thought the end of the world had come. He was a painter—and engraver. I had a great fondness for him. I used to go and see him, in the asylum. I'd take him by the hand and drag him to the window. Look! There! All that rising corn! And there! Look! The sails of the herring fleet! All that loveliness!
(Pause.)
He'd snatch away his hand and go back into his corner. Appalled. All he had seen was ashes.
(Pause.)
He alone had been spared.
(Pause.)
Forgotten.
(Pause.)
It appears the case is . . . was not so . . . so unusual.

CLOV:

A madman? When was that?

HAMM:

Oh way back, way back, you weren't in the land of the living.

CLOV:

God be with the days!
(Pause. Hamm raises his toque.)

HAMM:

I had a great fondness for him.
(Pause. He puts on his toque again.)
He was a painter—and engraver.

CLOV:

There are so many terrible things.

HAMM:

No, no, there are not so many now.

44

(Pause.)
Clov!

CLOV:
Yes.

HAMM:
Do you not think this has gone on long enough?

CLOV:
Yes!
(Pause.)
What?

HAMM:
This . . . this . . . thing.

CLOV:
I've always thought so.
(Pause.)
You not?

HAMM *(gloomily)*:
Then it's a day like any other day.

CLOV:
As long as it lasts.
(Pause.)
All life long the same inanities.

HAMM:
I can't leave you.

CLOV:
I know. And you can't follow me.
(Pause.)

HAMM:
If you leave me how shall I know?

CLOV *(briskly)*:
Well you simply whistle me and if I don't come running it means I've left you.
(Pause.)

HAMM:
You won't come and kiss me goodbye?

45

CLOV:
  Oh I shouldn't think so.
  (Pause.)

HAMM:
  But you might be merely dead in your kitchen.

CLOV:
  The result would be the same.

HAMM:
  Yes, but how would I know, if you were merely dead in your kitchen?

CLOV:
  Well . . . sooner or later I'd start to stink.

HAMM:
  You stink already. The whole place stinks of corpses.

CLOV:
  The whole universe.

HAMM *(angrily)*:
  To hell with the universe.
  (Pause.)
  Think of something.

CLOV:
  What?

HAMM:
  An idea, have an idea.
  (Angrily.)
  A bright idea!

CLOV:
  Ah good.
  (He starts pacing to and fro, his eyes fixed on the ground, his hands behind his back. He halts.)
  The pains in my legs! It's unbelievable! Soon I won't be able to think any more.

HAMM:
  You won't be able to leave me.

46

(Clov resumes his pacing.)
What are you doing?

CLOV:
Having an idea.
(He paces.)
Ah!
(He halts.)

HAMM:
What a brain!
(Pause.)
Well?

CLOV:
Wait!
(He meditates. Not very convinced.)
Yes . . .
(Pause. More convinced.)
Yes!
(He raises his head.)
I have it! I set the alarm.
(Pause.)

HAMM:
This is perhaps not one of my bright days, but frankly—

CLOV:
You whistle me. I don't come. The alarm rings. I'm gone. It
doesn't ring. I'm dead.
(Pause.)

HAMM:
Is it working?
(Pause. Impatiently.)
The alarm, is it working?

CLOV:
Why wouldn't it be working?

HAMM:
Because it's worked too much.

CLOV:
But it's hardly worked at all.

47

HAMM (*angrily*):
Then because it's worked too little!

CLOV:
I'll go and see.
(*Exit Clov. Brief ring of alarm off. Enter Clov with alarm-clock. He holds it against Hamm's ear and releases alarm. They listen to it ringing to the end. Pause.*)
Fit to wake the dead! Did you hear it?

HAMM:
Vaguely.

CLOV:
The end is terrific!

HAMM:
I prefer the middle.
(*Pause.*)
Is it not time for my pain-killer?

CLOV:
No!
(*He goes to door, turns.*)
I'll leave you.

HAMM:
It's time for my story. Do you want to listen to my story.

CLOV:
No.

HAMM:
Ask my father if he wants to listen to my story.
(*Clov goes to bins, raises the lid of Nagg's, stoops, looks into it. Pause. He straightens up.*)

CLOV:
He's asleep.

HAMM:
Wake him.
(*Clov stoops, wakes Nagg with the alarm. Unintelligible words. Clov straightens up.*)

48

CLOV:
    He doesn't want to listen to your story.

HAMM:
    I'll give him a bon-bon.
    (Clov stoops. As before.)

CLOV:
    He wants a sugar-plum.

HAMM:
    He'll get a sugar-plum.
    (Clov stoops. As before.)

CLOV:
    It's a deal.
    (He goes towards door. Nagg's hands appear, gripping the rim. Then the head emerges. Clov reaches door, turns.)
    Do you believe in the life to come?

HAMM:
    Mine was always that.
    (Exit Clov.)
    Got him that time!

NAGG:
    I'm listening.

HAMM:
    Scoundrel! Why did you engender me?

NAGG:
    I didn't know.

HAMM:
    What? What didn't you know?

NAGG:
    That it'd be you.
    (Pause.)
    You'll give me a sugar-plum?

HAMM:
    After the audition.

NAGG:
    You swear?

HAMM:
  Yes.

NAGG:
  On what?

HAMM:
  My honor.
  (Pause. They laugh heartily.)

NAGG:
  Two.

HAMM:
  One.

NAGG:
  One for me and one for—

HAMM:
  One! Silence!
  (Pause.)
  Where was I?
  (Pause. Gloomily.)
  It's finished, we're finished.
  (Pause.)
  Nearly finished.
  (Pause.)
  There'll be no more speech.
  (Pause.)
  Something dripping in my head, ever since the fontanelles.
  (Stifled hilarity of Nagg.)
  Splash, splash, always on the same spot.
  (Pause.)
  Perhaps it's a little vein.
  (Pause.)
  A little artery.
  (Pause. More animated.)
  Enough of that, it's story time, where was I?
  (Pause. Narrative tone.)
  The man came crawling towards me, on his belly. Pale, wonderfully pale and thin, he seemed on the point of—

50

(Pause. Normal tone.)
No, I've done that bit.
(Pause. Narrative tone.)
I calmly filled my pipe—the meerschaum, lit it with . . . let us say a vesta, drew a few puffs. Aah!
(Pause.)
Well, what is it *you* want?
(Pause.)
It was an extra-ordinarily bitter day, I remember, zero by the thermometer. But considering it was Christmas Eve there was nothing . . . extra-ordinary about that. Seasonable weather, for once in a way.
(Pause.)
Well, what ill wind blows you my way? He raised his face to me, black with mingled dirt and tears.
(Pause. Normal tone.)
That should do it.
(Narrative tone.)
No no, don't look at me, don't look at me. He dropped his eyes and mumbled something, apologies I presume.
(Pause.)
I'm a busy man, you know, the final touches, before the festivities, you know what it is.
(Pause. Forcibly.)
Come on now, what is the object of this invasion?
(Pause.)
It was a glorious bright day, I remember, fifty by the heliometer, but already the sun was sinking down into the . . . down among the dead.
(Normal tone.)
Nicely put, that.
(Narrative tone.)
Come on now, come on, present your petition and let me resume my labors.
(Pause. Normal tone.)
There's English for you. Ah well . . .
(Narrative tone.)

51

It was then he took the plunge. It's my little one, he said. Tsstss, a little one, that's bad. My little boy, he said, as if the sex mattered. Where did he come from? He named the hole. A good half-day, on horse. What are you insinuating? That the place is still inhabited? No no, not a soul, except himself and the child—assuming he existed. Good. I enquired about the situation at Kov, beyond the gulf. Not a sinner. Good. And you expect me to believe you have left your little one back there, all alone, and alive into the bargain? Come now!
(Pause.)
It was a howling wild day, I remember, a hundred by the anenometer. The wind was tearing up the dead pines and sweeping them . . . away.
(Pause. Normal tone.)
A bit feeble, that.
(Narrative tone.)
Come on, man, speak up, what is you want from me, I have to put up my holly.
(Pause.)
Well to make it short it finally transpired that what he wanted from me was . . . bread for his brat? Bread? But I have no bread, it doesn't agree with me. Good. Then perhaps a little corn?
(Pause. Normal tone.)
That should do it.
(Narrative tone.)
Corn, yes, I have corn, it's true, in my granaries. But use your head. I give you some corn, a pound, a pound and a half, you bring it back to your child and you make him—if he's still alive—a nice pot of porridge,
(Nagg reacts)
a nice pot and a half of porridge, full of nourishment. Good. The colors come back into his little cheeks—perhaps. And then?
(Pause.)
I lost patience.

52

(Violently.)
Use your head, can't you, use your head, you're on earth, there's no cure for that!
(Pause.)
It was an exceedingly dry day, I remember, zero by the hygrometer. Ideal weather, for my lumbago.
(Pause. Violently.)
But what in God's name do you imagine? That the earth will awake in spring? That the rivers and seas will run with fish again? That there's manna in heaven still for imbeciles like you?
(Pause.)
Gradually I cooled down, sufficiently at least to ask him how long he had taken on the way. Three whole days. Good. In what condition he had left the child. Deep in sleep.
(Forcibly.)
But deep in what sleep, deep in what sleep already?
(Pause.)
Well to make it short I finally offered to take him into my service. He had touched a chord. And then I imagined already that I wasn't much longer for this world.
(He laughs. Pause.)
Well?
(Pause.)
Well? Here if you were careful you might die a nice natural death, in peace and comfort.
(Pause.)
Well?
(Pause.)
In the end he asked me would I consent to take in the child as well—if he were still alive.
(Pause.)
It was the moment I was waiting for.
(Pause.)
Would I consent to take in the child . . .
(Pause.)
I can see him still, down on his knees, his hands flat on the

53

ground, glaring at me with his mad eyes, in defiance of my wishes.

(Pause. Normal tone.)

I'll soon have finished with this story.

(Pause.)

Unless I bring in other characters.

(Pause.)

But where would I find them?

(Pause.)

Where would I look for them?

(Pause. He whistles. Enter Clov.)

Let us pray to God.

NAGG:

Me sugar-plum!

CLOV:

There's a rat in the kitchen!

HAMM:

A rat! Are there still rats?

CLOV:

In the kitchen there's one.

HAMM:

And you haven't exterminated him?

CLOV:

Half. You disturbed us.

HAMM:

He can't get away?

CLOV:

No.

HAMM:

You'll finish him later. Let us pray to God.

CLOV:

Again!

NAGG:

Me sugar-plum!

HAMM:
    God first!
    (Pause.)
    Are you right?

CLOV *(resigned)*:
    Off we go.

HAMM *(to Nagg)*:
    And you?

NAGG *(clasping his hands, closing his eyes, in a gabble)*:
    Our Father which art—

HAMM:
    Silence! In silence! Where are your manners?
    (Pause.)
    Off we go.
    (Attitudes of prayer. Silence. Abandoning his attitude, discouraged.)
    Well?

CLOV *(abandoning his attitude)*:
    What a hope! And you?

HAMM:
    Sweet damn all!
    (To Nagg.)
    And you?

NAGG:
    Wait!
    (Pause. Abandoning his attitude.)
    Nothing doing!

HAMM:
    The bastard! He doesn't exist!

CLOV:
    Not yet.

NAGG:
    Me sugar-plum!

HAMM:
    There are no more sugar-plums!

55

(Pause.)

NAGG:

It's natural. After all I'm your father. It's true if it hadn't been me it would have been someone else. But that's no excuse.
(Pause.)
Turkish Delight, for example, which no longer exists, we all know that, there is nothing in the world I love more. And one day I'll ask you for some, in return for a kindness, and you'll promise it to me. One must live with the times.
(Pause.)
Whom did you call when you were a tiny boy, and were frightened, in the dark? Your mother? No. Me. We let you cry. Then we moved you out of earshot, so that we might sleep in peace.
(Pause.)
I was asleep, as happy as a king, and you woke me up to have me listen to you. It wasn't indispensable, you didn't really need to have me listen to you.
(Pause.)
I hope the day will come when you'll really need to have me listen to you, and need to hear my voice, any voice.
(Pause.)
Yes, I hope I'll live till then, to hear you calling me like when you were a tiny boy, and were frightened, in the dark, and I was your only hope.
(Pause. Nagg knocks on lid of Nell's bin. Pause.)
Nell!
(Pause. He knocks louder. Pause. Louder.)
Nell!
(Pause. Nagg sinks back into his bin, closes the lid behind him. Pause.)

HAMM:

Our revels now are ended.
(He gropes for the dog.)
The dog's gone.

CLOV:

He's not a real dog, he can't go.

HAMM (groping):
  He's not there.

CLOV:
  He's lain down.

HAMM:
  Give him up to me.
  (Clov picks up the dog and gives it to Hamm. Hamm holds it in his
  arms. Pause. Hamm throws away the dog.)
  Dirty brute!
  (Clov begins to pick up the objects lying on the ground.)
  What are you doing?

CLOV:
  Putting things in order.
  (He straightens up. Fervently.)
  I'm going to clear everything away!
  (He starts picking up again.)

HAMM:
  Order!

CLOV (straightening up):
  I love order. It's my dream. A world where all would be silent
  and still and each thing in its last place, under the last dust.
  (He starts picking up again.)

HAMM (exasperated):
  What in God's name do you think you are doing?

CLOV (straightening up):
  I'm doing my best to create a little order.

HAMM:
  Drop it!
  (Clov drops the objects he has picked up.)

CLOV:
  After all, there or elsewhere.
  (He goes towards door.)

HAMM (irritably):
  What's wrong with your feet?

CLOV:
   My feet?

HAMM:
   Tramp! Tramp!

CLOV:
   I must have put on my boots.

HAMM:
   Your slippers were hurting you?
   (Pause.)

CLOV:
   I'll leave you.

HAMM:
   No!

CLOV:
   What is there to keep me here?

HAMM:
   The dialogue.
   (Pause.)
   I've got on with my story.
   (Pause.)
   I've got on with it well.
   (Pause. Irritably.)
   Ask me where I've got to.

CLOV:
   Oh, by the way, your story?

HAMM *(surprised)*:
   What story?

CLOV:
   The one you've been telling yourself all your days.

HAMM:
   Ah you mean my chronicle?

CLOV:
   That's the one.
   (Pause.)

58

HAMM (angrily):
Keep going, can't you, keep going!

CLOV:
You've got on with it, I hope.

HAMM (modestly):
Oh not very far, not very far.
(He sighs.)
There are days like that, one isn't inspired.
(Pause.)
Nothing you can do about it, just wait for it to come.
(Pause.)
No forcing, no forcing, it's fatal.
(Pause.)
I've got on with it a little all the same.
(Pause.)
Technique, you know.
(Pause. Irritably.)
I say I've got on with it a little all the same.

CLOV (admiringly):
Well I never! In spite of everything you were able to get
on with it!

HAMM (modestly):
Oh not very far, you know, not very far, but nevertheless,
better than nothing.

CLOV:
Better than nothing! Is it possible?

HAMM:
I'll tell you how it goes. He comes crawling on his belly—

CLOV:
Who?

HAMM:
What?

CLOV:
Who do you mean, he?

59

HAMM:
Who do I mean! Yet another.

CLOV:
Ah him! I wasn't sure.

HAMM:
Crawling on his belly, whining for bread for his brat. He's offered a job as gardener. Before—
(Clov bursts out laughing.)
What is there so funny about that?

CLOV:
A job as gardener!

HAMM:
Is that what tickles you?

CLOV:
It must be that.

HAMM:
It wouldn't be the bread?

CLOV:
Or the brat.
(Pause.)

HAMM:
The whole thing is comical, I grant you that. What about having a good guffaw the two of us together?

CLOV *(after reflection)*:
I couldn't guffaw again today.

HAMM *(after reflection)*:
Nor I.
(Pause.)
I continue then. Before accepting with gratitude he asks if he may have his little boy with him.

CLOV:
What age?

HAMM:
Oh tiny.

60

CLOV:
  He would have climbed the trees.

HAMM:
  All the little odd jobs.

CLOV:
  And then he would have grown up.

HAMM:
  Very likely.
  (Pause.)

CLOV:
  Keep going, can't you, keep going!

HAMM:
  That's all. I stopped there.
  (Pause.)

CLOV:
  Do you see how it goes on.

HAMM:
  More or less.

CLOV:
  Will it not soon be the end?

HAMM:
  I'm afraid it will.

CLOV:
  Pah! You'll make up another.

HAMM:
  I don't know.
  (Pause.)
  I feel rather drained.
  (Pause.)
  The prolonged creative effort.
  (Pause.)
  If I could drag myself down to the sea! I'd make a pillow of
  sand for my head and the tide would come.

CLOV:
There's no more tide.
(Pause.)

HAMM:
Go and see is she dead.
(Clov goes to bins, raises the lid of Nell's, stoops, looks into it. Pause.)

CLOV:
Looks like it.
(He closes the lid, straightens up. Hamm raises his toque. Pause. He puts it on again.)

HAMM *(with his hand to his toque)*:
And Nagg?
(Clov raises lid of Nagg's bin, stoops, looks into it. Pause.)

CLOV:
Doesn't look like it.
(He closes the lid, straightens up.)

HAMM *(letting go his toque)*:
What's he doing?
(Clov raises lid of Nagg's bin, stoops, looks into it. Pause.)

CLOV:
He's crying.
(He closes lid, straightens up.)

HAMM:
Then he's living.
(Pause.)
Did you ever have an instant of happiness?

CLOV:
Not to my knowledge.
(Pause.)

HAMM:
Bring me under the window.
(Clov goes towards chair.)
I want to feel the light on my face.
(Clov pushes chair.)
Do you remember, in the beginning, when you took me for

62

a turn? You used to hold the chair too high. At every step
you nearly tipped me out.
(With senile quaver.)
Ah great fun, we had, the two of us, great fun.
(Gloomily.)
And then we got into the way of it.
(Clov stops the chair under window right.)
There already?
(Pause. He tilts back his head.)
Is it light?

CLOV:
It isn't dark.

HAMM *(angrily)*:
I'm asking you is it light.

CLOV:
Yes.
(Pause.)

HAMM:
The curtain isn't closed?

CLOV:
No.

HAMM:
What window is it?

CLOV:
The earth.

HAMM:
I knew it!
(Angrily.)
But there's no light there! The other!
(Clov pushes chair towards window left.)
The earth!
Clov stops the chair under window left. Hamm tilts back his head.)
That's what I call light!
(Pause.)
Feels like a ray of sunshine.

63

(Pause.)
No?

CLOV:
No.

HAMM:
It isn't a ray of sunshine I feel on my face?

CLOV:
No.
(Pause.)

HAMM:
Am I very white?
(Pause. Angrily.)
I'm asking you am I very white!

CLOV:
Not more so than usual.
(Pause.)

HAMM:
Open the window.

CLOV:
What for?

HAMM:
I want to hear the sea.

CLOV:
You wouldn't hear it.

HAMM:
Even if you opened the window?

CLOV:
No.

HAMM:
Then it's not worth while opening it?

CLOV:
No.

HAMM (*violently*):
　Then open it!
　(*Clov gets up on the ladder, opens the window. Pause.*)

　Have you opened it?

CLOV:
　Yes.
　(*Pause.*)

HAMM:
　You swear you've opened it?

CLOV:
　Yes.
　(*Pause.*)

HAMM:
　Well. . . !
　(*Pause.*)
　It must be very calm.
　(*Pause. Violently.*)
　I'm asking you is it very calm!

CLOV:
　Yes.

HAMM:
　It's because there are no more navigators.
　(*Pause.*)
　You haven't much conversation all of a sudden. Do you not
　feel well?

CLOV:
　I'm cold.

HAMM:
　What month are we?
　(*Pause.*)
　Close the window, we're going back.
　(*Clov closes the window, gets down, pushes the chair back to its place,
　remains standing behind it, head bowed.*)
　Don't stay there, you give me the shivers!
　(*Clov returns to his place beside the chair.*)

Father!
(Pause. Louder.)
Father!
(Pause.)
Go and see did he hear me.
(Clov goes to Nagg's bin, raises the lid, stoops. Uninitelligible words. Clov straightens up.)

CLOV:
Yes.

HAMM:
Both times?
(Clov stoops. As before.)

CLOV:
Once only.

HAMM:
The first time or the second?
(Clov stoops. As before.)

CLOV:
He doesn't know.

HAMM:
It must have been the second.

CLOV:
We'll never know.
(He closes lid.)

HAMM:
Is he still crying?

CLOV:
No.

HAMM:
The dead go fast.
(Pause.)
What's he doing?

CLOV:
Sucking his biscuit.

HAMM:
  Life goes on.
  (Clov returns to his place beside the chair.)
  Give me a rug, I'm freezing.

CLOV:
  There are no more rugs.
  (Pause.)

HAMM:
  Kiss me.
  (Pause.)
  Will you not kiss me?

CLOV:
  No.

HAMM:
  On the forehead.

CLOV:
  I won't kiss you anywhere.
  (Pause.)

HAMM *(holding out his hand)*:
  Give me your hand at least.
  (Pause.)
  Will you not give me your hand?

CLOV:
  I won't touch you.
  (Pause.)

HAMM:
  Give me the dog.
  (Clov looks round for the dog.)
  No!

CLOV:
  Do you not want your dog?

HAMM:
  No.

67

CLOV:
    Then I'll leave you.

HAMM *(head bowed, absently)*:
    That's right.
    (Clov goes to door, turns.)

CLOV:
    If I don't kill that rat he'll die.

HAMM *(as before)*:
    That's right.
    (Exit Clov. Pause.)
    Me to play.
    (He takes out his handkerchief, unfolds it, holds it spread out before him.)
    We're getting on.
    (Pause.)
    You weep, and weep, for nothing, so as not to laugh, and little by little . . . you begin to grieve.
    (He folds the handkerchief, puts it back in his pocket, raises his head.)
    All those I might have helped.
    (Pause.)
    Helped!
    (Pause.)
    Saved.
    (Pause.)
    Saved!
    (Pause.)
    The place was crawling with them!
    (Pause. Violently.)
    Use your head, can't you, use your head, you're on earth, there's no cure for that!
    (Pause.)
    Get out of here and love one another! Lick your neighbor as yourself!
    (Pause. Calmer.)
    When it wasn't bread they wanted it was crumpets.
    (Pause. Violently.)

Out of my sight and back to your petting parties!
(Pause.)
All that, all that!
(Pause.)
Not even a real dog!
(Calmer.)
The end is in the beginning and yet you go on.
(Pause.)
Perhaps I could go on with my story, end it and begin another.
(Pause.)
Perhaps I could throw myself out on the floor.
(He pushes himself painfully off his seat, falls back again.)
Dig my nails into the cracks and drag myself forward with my fingers.
(Pause.)
It will be the end and there I'll be, wondering what can have brought it on and wondering what can have . . .
(he hesitates)
. . . why it was so long coming.
(Pause.)
There I'll be, in the old shelter, alone against the silence and . . .
(he hesitates)
. . . the stillness. If I can hold my peace, and sit quiet, it will be all over with sound, and motion, all over and done with.
(Pause.)
I'll have called my father and I'll have called my . . .
(he hesitates)
. . . my son. And even twice, or three times, in case they shouldn't have heard me, the first time, or the second.
(Pause.)
I'll say to myself, He'll come back.
(Pause.)
And then?
(Pause.)
And then?
(Pause.)

He couldn't, he has gone too far.
(Pause.)
And then?
(Pause. Very agitated.)
All kinds of fantasies! That I'm being watched! A rat! Steps!
Breath held and then . . .
(He breathes out.)
Then babble, babble, words, like the solitary child who turns
himself into children, two, three, so as to be together, and
whisper together, in the dark.
(Pause.)
Moment upon moment, pattering down, like the millet grains
of . . .
(he hesitates)
. . . that old Greek, and all life long you wait for that to mount
up to a life.
(Pause. He opens his mouth to continue, renounces.)
Ah let's get it over!
(He whistles. Enter Clov with alarm-clock. He halts beside the chair.)
What? Neither gone nor dead?

CLOV:
In spirit only.

HAMM:
Which?

CLOV:
Both.

HAMM:
Gone from me you'd be dead.

CLOV:
And vice versa.

HAMM:
Outside of here it's death!
(Pause.)
And the rat?

CLOV:
   He's got away.

HAMM:
   He can't go far.
   (Pause. Anxious.)
   Eh?

CLOV:
   He doesn't need to go far.
   (Pause.)

HAMM:
   Is it not time for my pain-killer?

CLOV:
   Yes.

HAMM:
   Ah! At last! Give it to me! Quick!
   (Pause.)

CLOV:
   There's no more pain-killer.
   (Pause.)

HAMM *(appalled)*:
   Good. . . !
   (Pause.)
   No more pain-killer!

CLOV:
   No more pain-killer. You'll never get any more pain-killer.
   (Pause.)

HAMM:
   But the little round box. It was full!

CLOV:
   Yes. But now it's empty.
   (Pause. Clov starts to move about the room. He is looking for a place to put down the alarm-clock.)

HAMM *(soft)*:
   What'll I do?

71

(Pause. In a scream.)
What'll I do?
(Clov sees the picture, takes it down, stands it on the floor with its face to the wall, hangs up the alarm-clock in its place.)
What are you doing?

CLOV:
Winding up.

HAMM:
Look at the earth.

CLOV:
Again!

HAMM:
Since it's calling to you.

CLOV:
Is your throat sore?
(Pause.)
Would you like a lozenge?
(Pause.)
No.
(Pause.)
Pity.
(Clov goes, humming, towards window right, halts before it, looks up at it.)

HAMM:
Don't sing.

CLOV *(turning towards Hamm)*:
One hasn't the right to sing any more?

HAMM:
No.

CLOV:
Then how can it end?

HAMM:
You want it to end?

72

CLOV:
   I want to sing.
HAMM:
   I can't prevent you.
   (Pause. Clov turns towards window right.)
CLOV:
   What did I do with that steps?
   (He looks around for ladder.)
   You didn't see that steps?
   (He sees it.)
   Ah, about time.
   (He goes towards window left.)
   Sometimes I wonder if I'm in my right mind. Then it passes
   over and I'm as lucid as before.
   (He gets up on ladder, looks out of window.)
   Christ, she's under water!
   (He looks.)
   How can that be?
   (He pokes forward his head, his hand above his eyes.)
   It hasn't rained.
   (He wipes the pane, looks. Pause.)
   Ah what a fool I am! I'm on the wrong side!
   (He gets down, takes a few steps towards window right.)
   Under water!
   (He goes back for ladder.)
   What a fool I am!
   (He carries ladder towards window right.)
   Sometimes I wonder if I'm in my right senses. Then it passes
   off and I'm as intelligent as ever.
   *(He sets down ladder under window right, gets up on it, looks out of
   window. He turns towards Hamm.)*
   Any particular sector you fancy? Or merely the whole thing?
HAMM:
   Whole thing.
CLOV:
   The general effect? Just a moment.
   (He looks out of window. Pause.)

73

HAMM:
  Clov.

CLOV (*absorbed*):
  Mmm.

HAMM:
  Do you know what it is?

CLOV (*as before*):
  Mmm.

HAMM:
  I was never there.
  (*Pause.*)
  Clov!

CLOV (*turning towards Hamm, exasperated*):
  What is it?

HAMM:
  I was never there.

CLOV:
  Lucky for you.
  (*He looks out of window.*)

HAMM:
  Absent, always. It all happened without me. I don't know
  what's happened.
  (*Pause.*)
  Do you know what's happened?
  (*Pause.*)
  Clov!

CLOV (*turning towards Hamm, exasperated*):
  Do you want me to look at this muckheap, yes or no?

HAMM:
  Answer me first.

CLOV:
  What?

HAMM:
Do you know what's happened?

CLOV:
When? Where?

HAMM (*violently*):
When! What's happened? Use your head, can't you! What has happened?

CLOV:
What for Christ's sake does it matter?
(*He looks out of window.*)

HAMM:
I don't know.
(*Pause. Clov turns towards Hamm.*)

CLOV (*harshly*):
When old Mother Pegg asked you for oil for her lamp and you told her to get out to hell, you knew what was happening then, no?
(*Pause.*)
You know what she died of, Mother Pegg? Of darkness.

HAMM (*feebly*):
I hadn't any.

CLOV (*as before*):
Yes, you had.
(*Pause.*)

HAMM:
Have you the glass?

CLOV:
No, it's clear enough as it is.

HAMM:
Go and get it.
(*Pause. Clov casts up his eyes, brandishes his fists. He loses balance, clutches on to the ladder. He starts to get down, halts.*)

CLOV:
There's one thing I'll never understand.

75

(He gets down.)
Why I always obey you. Can you explain that to me?

HAMM:
No. . . . Perhaps it's compassion.
(Pause.)
A kind of great compassion.
(Pause.)
Oh you won't find it easy, you won't find it easy.
(Pause. Clov begins to move about the room in search of the telescope.)

CLOV:
I'm tired of our goings on, very tired.
(He searches.)
You're not sitting on it?
(He moves the chair, looks at the place where it stood, resumes his search.)

HAMM *(anguished)*:
Don't leave me there!
(Angrily Clov restores the chair to its place.)
Am I right in the center?

CLOV:
You'd need a microscope to find this—
(He sees the telescope.)
Ah, about time.
(He picks up the telescope, gets up on the ladder, turns the telescope on the without.)

HAMM:
Give me the dog.

CLOV *(looking)*:
Quiet!

HAMM *(angrily)*:
Give me the dog!
(Clov drops the telescope, clasps his hands to his head. Pause. He gets down precipitately, looks for the dog, sees it, picks it up, hastens towards Hamm and strikes him violently on the head with the dog.)

76

CLOV:
    There's your dog for you!
    (The dog falls to the ground. Pause.)

HAMM:
    He hit me!

CLOV:
    You drive me mad, I'm mad!

HAMM:
    If you must hit me, hit me with the axe.
    (Pause.)
    Or with the gaff, hit me with the gaff. Not with the dog. With
    the gaff. Or with the axe.
    (Clov picks up the dog and gives it to Hamm who takes it in his arms.)

CLOV *(imploringly)*:
    Let's stop playing!

HAMM:
    Never!
    (Pause.)
    Put me in my coffin.

CLOV:
    There are no more coffins.

HAMM:
    Then let it end!
    (Clov goes towards ladder.)
    With a bang!
    *(Clov gets up on ladder, gets down again, looks for telescope, sees it,
    picks it up, gets up ladder, raises telescope.)*
    Of darkness! And me? Did anyone ever have pity on me?

CLOV *(lowering the telescope, turning towards Hamm)*:
    What?
    (Pause.)
    Is it me you're referring to?

HAMM *(angrily)*:
    An aside, ape! Did you never hear an aside before?

(Pause.)
I'm warming up for my last soliloquy.

CLOV:
I warn you. I'm going to look at this filth since it's an order. But it's the last time.
(He turns the telescope on the without.)
Let's see.
(He moves the telescope.)
Nothing . . . nothing . . . good . . . good . . .nothing . . . goo—
(He starts, lowers the telescope, examines it, turns it again on the without. Pause.)
Bad luck to it!

HAMM:
More complications!
(Clov gets down.)
Not an underplot, I trust.
(Clov moves ladder nearer window, gets up on it, turns telescope on the without.)

CLOV *(dismayed)*:
Looks like a small boy!

HAMM *(sarcastic)*:
A small . . . boy!

CLOV:
I'll go and see.
(He gets down, drops the telescope, goes towards door, turns.)
I'll take the gaff.
(He looks for the gaff, sees it, picks it up, hastens towards door.)

HAMM:
No!
(Clov halts.)

CLOV:
No? A potential procreator?

HAMM:
If he exists he'll die there or he'll come here. And if he doesn't
. . .

(Pause.)

CLOV:

You don't believe me? You think I'm inventing?
(Pause.)

HAMM:

It's the end, Clov, we've come to the end. I don't need you
any more.
(Pause.)

CLOV:

Lucky for you.
(He goes towards door.)

HAMM:

Leave me the gaff.
*(Clov gives him the gaff, goes towards door, halts, looks at alarm-clock,
takes it down, looks round for a better place to put it, goes to bins,
puts it on lid of Nagg's bin. Pause.)*

CLOV:

I'll leave you.
(He goes towards door.)

HAMM:

Before you go . . .
(Clov halts near door.)
. . . say something.

CLOV:

There is nothing to say.

HAMM:

A few words . . . to ponder . . . in my heart.

CLOV:

Your heart!

HAMM:

Yes .
(Pause. Forcibly.)
Yes!
(Pause.)

With the rest, in the end, the shadows, the murmurs, all the trouble, to end up with.
(Pause.)
Clov. . . . He never spoke to me. Then, in the end, before he went, without my having asked him, he spoke to me. He said . . .

CLOV *(despairingly)*:
Ah. . . !

HAMM:
Something . . . from your heart.

CLOV:
My heart!

HAMM:
A few words . . . from your heart.
(Pause.)

CLOV *(fixed gaze, tonelessly, towards auditorium)*:
They said to me, That's love, yes, yes, not a doubt, now you see how—

HAMM:
Articulate!

CLOV *(as before)*:
How easy it is. They said to me, That's friendship, yes, yes, no question, you've found it. They said to me, Here's the place, stop, raise your head and look at all that beauty. That order! They said to me, Come now, you're not a brute beast, think upon these things and you'll see how all becomes clear. And simple! They said to me, What skilled attention they get, all these dying of their wounds.

HAMM:
Enough!

CLOV *(as before)*:
I say to myself—sometimes, Clov, you must learn to suffer better than that if you want them to weary of punishing you

80

—one day. I say to myself—sometimes, Clov, you must be there better than that if you want them to let you go—one day. But I feel too old, and too far, to form new habits. Good, it'll never end, I'll never go.

(Pause.)

Then one day, suddenly, it ends, it changes, I don't understand, it dies, or it's me, I don't understand, that either. I ask the words that remain—sleeping, waking, morning, evening. They have nothing to say.

(Pause.)

I open the door of the cell and go. I am so bowed I only see my feet, if I open my eyes, and between my legs a little trail of black dust. I say to myself that the earth is extinguished, though I never saw it lit.

(Pause.)

It's easy going.

(Pause.)

When I fall I'll weep for happiness.

(Pause. He goes towards door.)

HAMM:
Clov!
(Clov halts, without turning.)
Nothing.
(Clov moves on.)
Clov!
(Clov halts, without turning.)

CLOV:
This is what we call making an exit.

HAMM:
I'm obliged to you, Clov. For your services.

CLOV *(turning, sharply)*:
Ah pardon, it's I am obliged to you.

HAMM:
It's we are obliged to each other.
(Pause. Clov goes towards door.)

81

One thing more.
(Clov halts.)
A last favor.
(Exit Clov.)
Cover me with the sheet.
(Long pause.)
No? Good.
(Pause.)
Me to play.
(Pause. Wearily.)
Old endgame lost of old, play and lose and have done with losing.
(Pause. More animated.)
Let me see.
(Pause.)
Ah yes!
(He tries to move the chair, using the gaff as before. Enter Clov, dressed for the road. Panama hat, tweed coat, raincoat over his arm, umbrella, bag. He halts by the door and stands there, impassive and motionless, his eyes fixed on Hamm, till the end. Hamm gives up.)
Good.
(Pause.)
Discard.
(He throws away the gaff, makes to throw away the dog, thinks better of it.)
Take it easy.
(Pause.)
And now?
(Pause.)
Raise hat.
(He raises his toque.)
Peace to our . . . arses.
(Pause.)
And put on again.
(He puts on his toque.)
Deuce.
(Pause. He takes off his glasses.)
Wipe.

(He takes out his handkerchief and, without unfolding it, wipes his glasses.)

And put on again.

(He puts on his glasses, puts back the handkerchief in his pocket.)

We're coming. A few more squirms like that and I'll call.

(Pause.)

A little poetry.

(Pause.)

You prayed—

(Pause. He corrects himself.)

You CRIED for night; it comes—

(Pause. He corrects himself.)

It FALLS: now cry in darkness.

(He repeats, chanting.)

You cried for night; it falls: now cry in darkness.

(Pause.)

Nicely put, that.

(Pause.)

And now?

(Pause.)

Moments for nothing, now as always, time was never and time is over, reckoning closed and story ended.

(Pause. Narrative tone.)

If he could have his child with him. . . .

(Pause.)

It was the moment I was waiting for.

(Pause.)

You don't want to abandon him? You want him to bloom while you are withering? Be there to solace your last million last moments?

(Pause.)

He doesn't realize, all he knows is hunger, and cold, and death to crown it all. But you! You ought to know what the earth is like, nowadays. Oh I put him before his responsibilities!

(Pause. Normal tone.)

Well, there we are, there I am, that's enough.

83

(He raises the whistle to his lips, hesitates, drops it. Pause.)

Yes, truly!

(He whistles. Pause. Louder. Pause.)

Good.

(Pause.)

Father!

(Pause. Louder.)

Father!

(Pause.)

Good.

(Pause.)

We're coming.

(Pause.)

And to end up with?

(Pause.)

Discard.

(He throws away the dog. He tears the whistle from his neck.)

With my compliments.

(He throws whistle towards auditorium. Pause. He sniffs. Soft.)

Clov!

(Long pause.)

No? Good.

(He takes out the handkerchief.)

Since that's the way we're playing it . . .

(he unfolds handkerchief)

. . . let's play it that way . . .

(he unfolds)

. . . and speak no more about it . . .

(he finishes unfolding)

. . . speak no more.

(He holds handkerchief spread out before him.)

Old stancher!

(Pause.)

You . . . remain.

(Pause. He covers his face with handkerchief, lowers his arms to armrests, remains motionless.)

(Brief tableau.)

Curtain

Act Without Words

A MIME FOR ONE PLAYER

Desert. Dazzling light.

The man is flung backwards on stage from right wing. He falls, gets up immediately, dusts himself, turns aside, reflects.

Whistle from right wing.

He reflects, goes out right.

Immediately flung back on stage he falls, gets up immediately, dusts himself, turns aside, reflects.

Whistle from left wing.

He reflects, goes out left.

Immediately flung back on stage he falls, gets up immediately, dusts himself, turns aside, reflects.

Whistle from left wing.

He reflects, goes towards left wing, hesitates, thinks better of it, halts, turns aside, reflects.

A little tree descends from flies, lands. It has a single bough some three yards from ground and at its summit a meager tuft of palms casting at its foot a circle of shadow.

He continues to reflect.

Whistle from above.

He turns, sees tree, reflects, goes to it, sits down in its shadow, looks at his hands.

A pair of tailor's scissors descends from flies, comes to rest before tree, a yard from ground.

He continues to look at his hands.

Whistle from above.

He looks up, sees scissors, takes them and starts to trim his nails.

The palms close like a parasol, the shadow disappears.

He drops scissors, reflects.

87

A tiny carafe, to which is attached a huge label inscribed WATER, descends from flies, comes to rest some three yards from ground.

He continues to reflect.

Whistle from above.

He looks up, sees carafe, reflects, gets up, goes and stands under it, tries in vain to reach it, renounces, turns aside, reflects.

A big cube descends from flies, lands.

He continues to reflect.

Whistle from above.

He turns, sees cube, looks at it, at carafe, reflects, goes to cube, takes it up, carries it over and sets it down under carafe, tests its stability, gets up on it, tries in vain to reach carafe, renounces, gets down, carries cube back to its place, turns aside, reflects.

A second smaller cube descends from flies, lands.

He continues to reflect.

Whistle from above.

He turns, sees second cube, looks at it, at carafe, goes to second cube, takes it up, carries it over and sets it down under carafe, tests its stability, gets up on it, tries in vain to reach carafe, renounces, gets down, takes up second cube to carry it back to its place, hesitates, thinks better of it, sets it down, goes to big cube, takes it up, carries it over and puts it on small one, tests their stability, gets up on them, the cubes collapse, he falls, gets up immediately, brushes himself, reflects.

He takes up small cube, puts it on big one, tests their stability, gets up on them and is about to reach carafe when it is pulled up a little way and comes to rest beyond his reach.

He gets down, reflects, carries cubes back to their place, one by one, turns aside, reflects.

A third still smaller cube descends from flies, lands.

He continues to reflect.

Whistle from above.

He turns, sees third cube, looks at it, reflects, turns aside, reflects.

The third cube is pulled up and disappears in flies.

Beside carafe a rope descends from flies, with knots to facilitate ascent.

He continues to reflect.

Whistle from above.

He turns, sees rope, reflects, goes to it, climbs up it and is about to reach carafe when rope is let out and deposits him back on ground.

He reflects, looks around for scissors, sees them, goes and picks them up, returns to rope and starts to cut it with scissors.

The rope is pulled up, lifts him off ground, he hangs on, succeeds in cutting rope, falls back on ground, drops scissors, falls, gets up again immediately, brushes himself, reflects.

The rope is pulled up quickly and disappears in flies.

With length of rope in his possession he makes a lasso with which he tries to lasso carafe.

The carafe is pulled up quickly and disappears in flies.

He turns aside, reflects.

He goes with lasso in his hand to tree, looks at bough, turns and looks at cubes, looks again at bough, drops lasso, goes to cubes, takes up small one, carries it over and sets it down under bough, goes back for big one, takes it up and carries it over under bough, makes to put it on small one, hesitates, thinks better of it, sets it down, takes up small one and puts it on big one, tests their stability, turns aside and stoops to pick up lasso.

89

The bough folds down against trunk.

He straightens up with lasso in his hand, turns and sees what has happened.

He drops lasso, turns aside, reflects.

He carries back cubes to their place, one by one, goes back for lasso, carries it over to cubes and lays it in a neat coil on small one.

He turns aside, reflects.

Whistle from right wing.

He reflects, goes out right.

Immediately flung back on stage he falls, gets up immediately, brushes himself, turns aside, reflects.

Whistle from left wing.

He does not move.

He looks at his hands, looks around for scissors, sees them, goes and picks them up, starts to trim his nails, stops, reflects, runs his finger along blade of scissors, goes and lays them on small cube, turns aside, opens his collar, frees his neck and fingers it.

The small cube is pulled up and disappears in flies, carrying away rope and scissors.

He turns to take scissors, sees what has happened.

He turns aside, reflects.

He goes and sits down on big cube.

The big cube is pulled from under him. He falls. The big cube is pulled up and disappears in flies.

He remains lying on his side, his face towards auditorium, staring before him.

The carafe descends from flies and comes to rest a few feet from his body.

He does not move.

Whistle from above.

He does not move.

The carafe descends further, dangles and plays about his face.

He does not move.

The carafe is pulled up and disappears in flies.

The bough returns to horizontal, the palms open, the shadow returns.

Whistle from above.

He does not move.

The tree is pulled up and disappears in flies.

He looks at his hands.

Curtain